MOTHING FIELD JOURNAL

Record moth sightings, dates, and locations

This journal belongs to:

_____
_____

© Dirty botany 2018

Date	Species	Location	★

Notes

Date	Species	Location	★

Notes

Date	Species	Location	★

Notes

Date	Species	Location	★

Notes

Date	Species	Location	★

Notes

Date	Species	Location	★

Notes

Date	Species	Location	★

Notes

Date	Species	Location	★

Notes

Date	Species	Location	★

Notes

Date	Species	Location	★

Notes

Date	Species	Location	★

Notes

Date	Species	Location	★

Notes

Date	Species	Location	★

Notes

Date	Species	Location	★

Notes

_____
_____
_____
_____
_____
_____
_____
_____

Date	Species	Location	★

Notes

Date	Species	Location	★

Notes

Date	Species	Location	★

Notes

Date	Species	Location	★

Notes

Date	Species	Location	★

Notes

Date	Species	Location	★

Notes

Date	Species	Location	★

Notes

Date	Species	Location	★

Notes

Date	Species	Location	★

Notes

Date	Species	Location	★

Notes

Date	Species	Location	★

Notes

Date	Species	Location	★

Notes

Date	Species	Location	★

Notes

Date	Species	Location	★

Notes

Date	Species	Location	★

Notes

Date	Species	Location	★

Notes

Date	Species	Location	★

Notes

Date	Species	Location	★

Notes

Date	Species	Location	★

Notes

Date	Species	Location	★

Notes

Date	Species	Location	★

Notes

Date	Species	Location	★

Notes

_____
_____
_____
_____
_____
_____
_____

Date	Species	Location	★

Notes

Date	Species	Location	★

Notes

Date	Species	Location	★

Notes

Date	Species	Location	★

Notes

Notes

Notes

Notes

Notes

Notes

Sketches

Sketches

Please see our Author Page on Amazon for more nature inspired journals and ledgers!

Printed in Great Britain
by Amazon